HEAVEN CAN BE HELL

PAT G'ORGE-WALKER

PAT G'ORGE-WALKER BOOKS

Heaven Can Be Hell © 2019 by Pat G'Orge-Walker

Published by Pat G'Orge-Walker

This story is a work of fiction. Names, characters, places, and incidents are products of the author's imagination or are used fictitiously and are not to be construed as real. Any resemblance to actual events, locales, organizations, or persons, living, dead or somewhere in between, is entirely coincidental.

All rights reserved. No part of this book may be reproduced in any form or by any means including electronic, mechanical, or photocopying or stored in a retrieval system without permission in writing from the publisher except by a reviewer who may quote brief passages to be included in a review.

Trade Paperback ISBN: 978-0-9660155-8-4

Cover designed by: Naleighna Kai for Woodson Creative Studio

Interior design by: Naleighna Kai for Woodson Creative Studio

ACKNOWLEDGMENTS

After losing the love of my life, my husband Rob in 2013 it took the wind out of me. Some probably thought I'd just given up and retreated into the shadows. I did.

I thank Kensington Books and my editor at Dafina, Selena James for not giving up on me.

However, if it were not for the determination of National and Best-Selling author/editor/publisher Lissa Woodson, aka Naleighna Kai, I would've somehow kept writing stories in my head and never put them on paper. Naleighna was the daily bane of my existence, the persistent Gatekeeper to my writing pen, (did I mention she was the pain in my tookus)... you get the point. And I love her for it.

The support from my NK Tribe Called Success and Inner Circle Tribe family is, without a doubt, the wind beneath my wings. Never have I been a part of such a phenomenal group of giving and supportive group of like-minded literary scribes. No one allowed to quit. No one was envious of another. The Tribe was and is still, tight.

As far as my story *Heaven Can Be Hell*. It is different from what I am expected to write. This story is Christian fiction for adults. This story was based upon some of my real experiences and let's just say, "I haven't been Saved all my life. I have done some "thangs." LOL.

Hope you will enjoy *Heaven Can Be Hell.*

CHAPTER 1

$\mathcal{A}$veric's head snapped upward at the annoying static sound that snatched him from preparing for his sermon.

"Be warned; all verified hell is about to visit you," Aunt Peaches blasted from the intercom.

"Say what?" Startled, the six-foot-five, thirty-five-year-old shot forward in his chair. The sudden movement caused him to scrape his knee against the side of the desk. He grimaced at the sudden bite of pain as he pressed the intercom's button. "Say that again."

Being out of breath and inhaling quickly caused a slight hiccup to escape in her excitement. She blurted in her signature rapid-fire and politically incorrect manner, "Well, nephew-pastor, it's a warm and lovely May afternoon, and I know you studying so you can preach everybody to Paradise come your turn next Sunday morning, especially since you figuring you gonna become senior pastor in a few weeks—"

Averic sighed his frustration. For a while, rumors were going around the church and town that his gossipy widowed aunt was looking for a new husband. Aunt Peaches, built like a rusty-colored beer keg, was seen in some of her pre-saved life hangouts trying to use her old fleshly equipment as unwanted collateral. He didn't want her feelings hurt or someone getting shot, since she was also a licensed concealed gun carrier. Feeling obligated, Averic hired her to be his assistant. And that's when the real fun began.

Today, he had promised to meet with Pastor's Aid Committee heads Mama Mae-Aye and Trustee Black Mack to discuss the upcoming retirement benefit for the current senior pastor. *I might as well pull out the checkbook. They're gonna tell me how cheap I am and that five thousand dollars couldn't buy a decent tablecloth.* He was sure that the Lord himself popped Tylenol every time those two old shysters complained. However, he still didn't appreciate his aunt's reference.

"Let me remind you again," Averic said slowly, still massaging his sore kneecap, "I don't want you comparing any meeting I have with our members to a session in Hell."

The sound of a small, exasperated gasp filtered through the intercom. Aunt Peaches lowered her voice, adding in a more respectful, yet reprimanding tone, "Well please forgive me, Wanna-be-a-Senior Pastor-elect-Reverend-Doctor-Averic Domingo. As your late mama's only sister and your once-favorite auntie, I was just tryin' to tell you that Mama Mae-Aye and Trustee Black Mack can't make their scheduled meeting."

"Seriously?" He could have stayed home and packed for his upcoming trip instead of traipsing across town to the church to get his feelings hurt in what was sure to be a geriatric beat down.

A chuckle quickly replaced the stern measure in Aunt Peaches' voice. "Actually, I overheard a conversation while I was in the second stall in the second-floor ladies' room."

Averic slapped a hand to his forehead harder than he had meant to. *The devil is a liar.* The last thing he wanted was that mental picture to accompany his aunt's confession.

"Ain't no secret that all kinds of truths and such can be learned from any second stall in the ladies' bathroom all over the world," she said, oblivious to the fact that she was making lunch an impossible thing. "Like I said, they're gonna go over to Shout Now Community Church for their Elders' Day celebration this evenin'."

"Thank you for all your *extra* info," Averic replied slowly, knowing from past conversations during Thanksgiving dinners, barbecues, and every other family-related occasion that it would be fruitless to remind her of her fondness for giving too much information. Instead, he replied, "Well, since they canceled and we've discussed not having any *hellish* meetings," he paused, making certain his point still carried, "and I don't have another meeting scheduled this afternoon, I'm leaving so I can get to the airport and make it to the Annual Honolulu Singles and Married Couples retreat in Hawaii for the next few days."

As a further reminder that she should not have tacked something else on his schedule, he added, "I hope to meet with Minister Craig during his Couples Retreat function."

"Hold up, I wouldn't exactly say you don't have any other meetings today," Aunt Peaches told him in a manner that suddenly sounded a bit more serious than necessary.

Averic froze in the middle of returning his documents to a manila folder. "What do you mean?"

"I mean, you can't go home because *now* you *do* have another meeting." Her high-pitched nasal voice returned as she cautioned, "It's someone who hasn't been here in a while. I guess she's overdue for a visit."

Peaches' voice betrayed her as a sudden snicker came over the intercom, masking her mocked concern.

Averic's eyes rolled in pure frustration. "Well, whoever *she* is, I don't have time to meet with her. I'm certainly not in the mood for any confusion right now. Let one of the deacons deal with whatever problem she has."

"Deacon Slipp," Aunt Peaches blurted. "He seen her first and he passed the word onto me. He may be about my age, but he's too old for this new-fangled mess younger folk bringing to the church. He said he knew trouble when he seen it and his power of discernment had told him that he wasn't missing no five-dollar Mighty Wing special at Church's Chunky Chicken to handle it."

The loud sound of Aunt Peaches' wheezing echoed. "So, it looks like you'd better *make* time, and as much as it pains me to say it, you gotta take a hit for the church's sanity team. Besides, you supposed to stay prayed-up." She lowered her voice. "I'd stay and sit in this particular meeting with you, but I ain't that saved yet."

Aunt Peaches' sometimes-zany remarks still managed to catch him off guard, but admitting something like that last part put him on notice. His nose twitched as though he could smell the always pleasant aroma of his Acqua Di Gio cologne fading, his plane ticket to Hawaii for three days disappearing into volcanic smoke, and the acrid smell of Hell's sulfur permeating the office air.

"Okay," he snapped. "Send whoever *she* is in here. It's my charge to keep. Who is it?"

"Glad you finally got around to asking because she's waiting inside the sanctuary. You ain't seen that heffa in a long time. I hoped you'd never see her again."

Choosing to ignore Aunt Peaches' devilish reference to someone being a "heffa," he replied, "Well, bring her inside, please. I really want to get out of here as soon as possible."

"Not as soon as you'll wanna be," Aunt Peaches replied angrily. "because it's your wife. I still can't figure out why her mama named that hellion Heaven."

CHAPTER 2

Heaven paced inside the newly remodeled sanctuary. Since it was Saturday, she hadn't expected many others to be at the church, but she was certain Averic would be. Spending most of his time within these walls was one of the reasons she had felt ignored. Not a good thing for a young marriage. Or for a woman who, despite convincing the outside world her life was first class, felt confined to coach when it came to her marriage. She could never move beyond her self-doubt, and her role in God's plan--if there ever was one.

Since arriving almost twenty minutes ago, Heaven had only laid eyes on one person. To her misfortune, it was a nosey old deacon. She was amused when the crypt-creeper first approached. His ill-fitting black suit, wrinkled tie, and wisps of thinning snow-white kinky hair —was enough to be held in contempt of not attending his own funeral in a timely fashion. And he smelled of musk and mold. His odor, which battled the sweet aroma of lavender-scented candles near the altar, almost sent Heaven out the sanctuary door. She had felt punished by his presence because all she'd asked was, "Do you know if Reverend Domingo is in his office?"

When the old deacon finally limped away, Heaven had quickly

made her way to a back pew in a far corner. As a teen in Anderson, South Carolina, the back pew was her comfort spot. Her father, the late Bishop Cornelius Foxx, couldn't see that far. She was seldom called on to pray or to sing when hidden among the hundreds of other church folk. She never liked doing what she didn't want to do, not even for her father. Now, for the past five years, before her marriage and during her separation, whatever church Heaven decided to grace —or threaten—with her presence, she still claimed the safety of the back pew.

Heaven checked her watch and quickly pulled a mirrored compact from a beige calfskin Fendi bag with her free hand. The harvest gold 2Jours bag, a thirtieth birthday gift she had given herself early last week, was a perfect match to the mustard and chocolate brown, boxed-designer dress and matching five-inch heels. With high heels and a size six figure, she always dressed so she would be as close to being mistaken for a professional model as possible

Before meeting Averic, she graduated from Clemson University in South Carolina, where she majored in marketing with a minor in commercial law. She loved learning shortcuts, legal or otherwise, when it came to manipulating business and human nature. Once she discovered there wasn't enough excitement in that part of the marketing world, and its sugar daddies were at a minimum, she searched for something that would satisfy her other interest in commercial law. A two-day trip to the Bahamas with an older Irish gentleman she'd met during a real estate law seminar came at the perfect time. He was her ticket off the Island of Boredom. Unfortunately for him, he was married. Fortunately for Heaven, he wanted his mega-rich wife kept uninformed.

Heaven had magically introduced her diamond blinged-out cell phone to him.

"I've been trying to break into the Graham and Taylor law firm so I can get ahead in commercial law," she'd told him. "It's in the building you own."

With one hand firmly on her hip, phone in the other, and her feet planted, she continued. "My family's only about fifty miles away should I need to call on my ex-con cousin, Buddha--"

The man quickly decided a quid pro quo was the appropriate payment.

As dishonest as the man was in his marriage, he kept his word. Heaven landed a position with the prestigious law firm in downtown Columbia, South Carolina. He was glad she hadn't made any threats when she learned she would start at entry level. However, her flirtatious enthusiasm and beauty kept her a step ahead of other law clerks who managed to show some decorum and dignity. Heaven kept her appearance call girl ready. While some of those other women merely *came to work*, Heaven made certain she *arrived* at work.

When it became an open secret that there weren't many boundaries Heaven wouldn't cross, the senior partners at Graham and Taylor sent her on unscheduled luncheon dates with prospective clients. Heaven's real job was to use her quick wit, beauty, and ability to be the "closer" on many lucrative contracts. She was definitely a "team player" if the client warranted a little *extra* attention. Her results always added to the firm's financial coffers. She didn't worry that she would never rise above the title of law clerk on paper, because she had a huge expense account, a company car, and the rent in her upscale condo was never late.

As well as things had gone at the law firm, Heaven's idea of real achievement—peace of mind—remained out of reach even after she'd met Averic. She'd begun making unreasonable demands from the managing partners at the firm. The company had reluctantly given her a six-month hiatus, to "rest," both mentally and physically, but not because they'd wanted to do it. Heaven had quietly threatened to write a "tell-all," and revealed she had incriminating receipts. She'd barely spoken her demands when they gave in, wanting her to keep her "pretty mouth shut."

Eventually, it didn't matter. And as with most of her bad decisions, she quit, not bothering to give a two-week notice. With a collective sigh of relief at having made her sign a non-disclosure agreement, the firm handed her a huge check on her way out the door. They were taking no chances.

But that was then.

Heaven's cell phone vibrated interrupting her thoughts and causing her to shudder. She sighed and chose to ignore it.

"Lord, I need a miracle." The words she suddenly whispered shook her to the core. She hadn't reached out to God in quite some time, and sitting on that pew she wasn't certain God would still be there for her. "I realize I was wrong to leave my husband, and I feel so incomplete without him. I let these church folk hurt me with their judgments, rumors." With her hands clasped she dropped her chin and began to sway in her seat. "Averic didn't stand up for me like he should've. I felt less than valuable as his wife." Heaven unclasped her hands, placed them in her lap before she continued. "You turned him into the servant *You* wanted. Couldn't you have made him the husband *I* needed?"

"Chill out, Heaven," she murmured as she raised her head, running her hand over the peaks of her copper-blonde ringlet haircut before straightening her shoulders as in defiance of the universe. "God didn't help you get Averic in the first place."

With no thought to being in a holy place, Heaven ran her small hands over her body from her ample breasts down to the high slit in her skirt. "It was all this."

This visit to see Averic, dressed in the same sexy flesh bait that snared him before, should work.

Despite her momentary bravado, her insolence faded as she whispered. "Lord, I know you need him." Heaven's eyes moistened with unshed tears as she again confessed to the large picture of Jesus hanging on the wall between the pews and the altar, "But I need him more. And, no disrespect, but I mean to get him again."

CHAPTER 3

*A*veric ran a hand through his hair while trying to stabilize whatever breath he had left. "Run that by me one more time."

"You heard me," Aunt Peaches quipped. "your ex-wife, Heaven."

At the sound of his estranged wife's name, Averic suddenly grabbed his other knee. Although uninjured, he was sure it was also in for a world of hurt. Heaven Domingo could definitely be Hell.

"Well, maybe she's not an ex yet," Aunt Peaches shot back, determined to finish her unwelcomed back-down-memory-lane rant, "but she sure needs to be. She's always been out of order. Fact is, folks still tossing shade behind ya back. Darn shame, especially with the way she sashayed into the women's conference on Waikiki beach all loud more than a few months after yawl was *secretly* dating. Half the women prayed the men would be struck temporarily blind. That heffa was wearin' two neon pink Band-Aids and tiny dental floss, trying to pass it off as a string bikini and such. And you certainly wasn't foolin' nobody. You was twitchin' like you were dancing the Wobble, acting like you was wantin' to be raptured up at that very second to avoid the embarrassment."

"That's enough!" Averic's voice rose as high as it would when he was in the spirit preaching, to no avail. Aunt Peaches' motor mouth was in full throttle, and no amount of imaginary brakes would stop her.

"—And Deacon Slipp said he didn't notice she was wearin' that expensive ring you emptied your bank account for, so I guess she over you and back on the hunt or auction block. Whatever they call it."

"Stop it, Aunt Peaches. She's still my wife." *Unfortunately.* "You're in God's house, and you should know better."

But the woman was not through.

"You think she came here might wantin' you to sign some divorce papers? I certainly hope so cause you could do better if you wasn't so uptight and telling folks what to do and not do in their own bedrooms." Her voice suddenly softened as she added, "I'm just telling you for the umpteenth time, 'cause I love you."

And he loved his aunt. She'd helped his father raise him after his mother died when he was only eleven years old. However, there were a few issues in their relationship once he graduated from college. Even more so when he became a minister at Free Will Assembly, but only after the fiasco with Heaven had died down.

That "love" for her nephew didn't last two seconds before she was back at it. "I know I keep sayin' it, but I still don't know why her mama named that hellish woman Heaven."

It took Averic a few seconds to realize that the intercom's silence meant Aunt Peaches had stopped her assault and thankfully hung up.

Averic leaned forward in his chair with his mouth slightly open as though trying to gulp a wisp of bravery. He then lifted his muscular arms, crossing them behind his head before falling back in his chair.

He remembered how much he'd loved watching Heaven's dark, long-lashed eyes peer out from the canvas of her heart-shaped face blessed with a flawless peaches-and-cream complexion. Her curvy frame woke his body, no matter how tired he felt. Fighting the urge to smile, he also remembered that every time she entered a room; her shape was a sure-fire money magnet.

"She could make the Pope rob a bank and still thank God the entire time in prison," Averic whispered.

The words barely left his mouth before Averic realized he was still in his study, supposedly a holy place. But he couldn't help it.

Averic suddenly pounded his fist on the desk. His spirituality had grown immensely after she'd abandoned him. He wasn't supposed to let Heaven's reappearance in his life, no matter how long or short it was, cause this kind of reaction.

Loosening another button from the top of his shirt, he quickly reached for his Bible, and it fell open to Proverbs 18:22—*He who finds a wife finds what is good and receives favor from the Lord*. Closing the Good Book quickly, but respectfully, Averic still felt otherwise.

Back then all the hounds chased this kind of Foxx.

"I just had to be the dumb something to catch Heaven and marry her," he whispered. "Now here it is eighteen months later, and I'm still catching Hell."

CHAPTER 4

*H*eaven had barely opened her compact when she spied Averic through the mirror entering the sanctuary's front door. She tilted her face, smiling with anticipation before disappointment set in. He suddenly stopped moving. Pursing her lips like an impatient child, she still couldn't look away. Averic's caramel complexion darkened until it appeared flushed. She then became amused as his piercing green eyes scanned the dimly lit sanctuary, looking obviously everywhere except where she sat.

He hasn't changed at all from our time in Hawaii.

Averic had the same unruly dark curly hair and well-toned muscular body that only a favorite son of Mother Nature could receive. Chiseled thighs embraced by a pair of barely loose blue jeans. Her body tingled as she scanned the same flesh-package that had attracted her when she first laid eyes on him. Despite his money and obvious well-educated mind, his physical appearance was still his best feature.

Without giving a second thought to the holiness of the place she now sat, Heaven ran her tongue over her lips, painted with MAC rose-colored lipstick, as if preparing for a delicious meal. She lowered her eyes slightly. *That man is still my kryptonite.*

Given what had happened almost two years ago, she shouldn't be surprised.

Heaven's eyes suddenly widened, and her body tensed slightly as she strummed those perfectly polished coral nails with diamond accents across the purse in her lap.

The collection had been barely taken up from the Annual Honolulu Single and Married Women's Conference, which she had attended with a friend who just had to hear a dynamic young preacher bring the Word. With nothing to do that night, Heaven tagged along.

The young preacher was everything her friend had said. He was a man much too well-toned, tall, and good looking to be seated in any church pulpit. More suited to a feature in a hot male stripper magazine, Averic Domingo had preached the women into a frenzy. He was straight out telling them never to allow any man, husband or otherwise, to abuse or use them sexually, mentally or in any other perverted method.

"Your body is God's temple," he'd told them. "Would you defile the temple of God?"

She'd found him a bit amusing because everything he'd said not to allow, she'd done with the greatest of ease and without regret. If she had her way, she would continue, with a little extra mind-blowing acrobatics on the side.

When the floor was opened for discussion, and he asked if anyone had questions, Heaven raised her hand.

"I'm a bit embarrassed to ask my question in front of so many people," she said with pretend shyness. "I'd rather ask you in private." She stopped long enough to see if he would give her an opening.

"I'll set aside a few minutes for consultation after, but I would need to get back to the conference attendees quickly."

Sounded about right.

Heaven followed him to a secluded area of the hotel lobby, pretending to straighten the slit in her red skirt that stopped just short of her mid-thigh with an exaggerated finger spread. She then wiped aside a pretend tear while she listed all the sexual acts she'd committed, all the while sizing him up for any latent inhibitions. She'd said she was earnest in wanting answers but wasn't sure which were abominations and which were forgivable.

Thirty minutes later, a gape-mouthed Averic was sweating profusely—

but not from the hot and humid Hawaiian weather. The conference all but forgotten, he and Heaven were on their way to a nearby hotel, suddenly thirsty for one another and not caring where or how much it took to quench it.

Less than an hour later, they were making love on the seventh-floor balcony of the Honolulu Princess Hotel. Both had indulged in a little too much Jack Daniels, despite his protests that he no longer drank. His refusals only elevated Heaven's desire to see how far she could push him. Every time he'd slide the glass away, she'd gently shove it back, kissing him deeply. In no time, they were naked. However, Averic's protests disappeared when Heaven pulled the handcuffs from her bag.

They did everything Averic had told the women at the conference not to do, and more. They'd even put several new twists to some of the "temple defilement" list of no-nos.

Several hours later, succumbing to Heaven and Jack Daniels, Averic was beyond normal drunk; he was almost comatose. Unfortunately for Heaven, she was still naked on the balcony cuffed to the railings. He had yet to wake from his drunken stupor. It was her bad luck that she wasn't released so she could use the bathroom. Cleanup on Aisle 7, Kmart shoppers.

Thinking about the best parts of that first time in Hawaii made Heaven tingle slightly. She closed her eyes again and collapsed slightly against the back of the pew, enjoying more of the exotic visit down memory lane ...

They couldn't hold their laughter any better than their liquor. She remembered Averic was afraid they'd be discovered. "I don't need a scandal attached to my ministry," he'd told her. It didn't matter because with hypocrisy in their routine, they continued to have a good laugh every time they snuck away over the next several nights after each conference meeting.

Snapping back to her current situation, she took a deep breath and clicked the compact shut. Her eyes again began that flirtatious dance as she gave Averic a lengthy once-over. She smoothed the hem of her dress to expose one of her best assets—long, shapely legs. Averic was two rows away by then, and her smile broadened, seemingly matching his own. His smile made him appear suddenly shy and inhibited.

His indiscretion cost him the appointment as pastor. Instead, the current pastor stayed on a while longer, allowing time for everything to sort itself out. Even if Averic's church, particularly his Aunt Peaches, chose to accept his repentance over their Hawaiian liaison, she knew better. She'd always felt it was stupid for him to confess and apologize for what had been natural for two people so sexually attracted to one another.

"Heaven."

She turned her head as Averic finally reached her. Heaven schooled her expression to appear neutral, not wanting to show a trace of excitement. She focused intensely as though he were prey.

Heaven purred, "It's me."

She took Averic's extended hand, disappointed he had welcomed her as though meeting for the first time. She flashed a white-on-white toothy smile and kissed the back of his hand.

Her displeasure was momentary when she listened to Averic stammer, "I ... I would've never guessed my, err, estranged wife would be my surprise visitor."

Heaven gently brushed Averic's hand aside and rose. She gave him no time to protest before she invited herself into his arms.

"Don't be so formal," she quipped, allowing her short, sassy, copper-blonde ringlets to rest a moment on his muscular chest. She tilted her head, allowing her lips to leave a slight stain on his shirt before lifting her head completely. "We were—and are— still married. That makes us too close for any formal handshake welcome."

Averic struggled to break the unexpected spell that silenced his tongue.

"So," he began in a low and hesitant voice while caressing the solid gold cross hanging around his neck. He grasped it tight enough to leave a print in his palm. He wouldn't look her in the face. The avoidance didn't last when his eyes finally met hers. "Heaven, what really brings you to Charleston?"

He leaned briefly against a nearby wall, then thought better of it and stood up straight.

Averic's lips parted, but no words came. His alternate version of reality was always a gut punch. The feelings that spread over his body let him know he still had no defense.

Lord help me.

Without thinking, he turned his head a little because a small movement was all he could make.

What does she want? How much will it cost me this time?

He didn't have much left to give. She'd taken away much of his dignity when she'd suddenly left. Even when she'd confessed that she didn't feel she was in the same league as most First Ladies, or that she was hardly the wife he deserved. He'd almost succumbed to despair just thinking about his Heaven being sampled by another man. Without some honest foundation in God, he might have tumbled into that abyss. *Why didn't I take her serious when she said she never felt good enough or accepted by the church? I shouldn't have told her to stop wearing revealing clothes or temper her words with Bible phrases or other stupid stuff. I wanted her one way at home and another in church. She wasn't ready.*

When she first left it caused him to question whether it was a real love for her that held him captive or the way she made him feel whenever they made love. It wasn't a question he felt he could take to God and get an answer, so he suffered and hoped to get over her.

Heaven's face almost gave way to a smirk, pleased she could still get to him. She was certain he might have pushed her away if she'd been one of his members who hugged him in that "certain way." She was also confident that he was probably still the same hypocrite she'd taken to paradise right after he'd preached the congregation happy. She'd done it on several occasions before and after they'd married.

With total control over her outward emotions, Heaven now took her time going over her plan. She hadn't sought out Averic after all this time to let her emotions consume her. That didn't mean she couldn't use this time to secretly enjoy the muscular arms that now held her. The strong biceps seemingly had a mind of their own. She could feel an inner purr arise deep within and she frowned while trying to fight it. Heaven felt hypnotized with a need for him, mingled with an outpouring of XXX-rated memories, despite the pews, the altar, and the pictures of the Lord displayed throughout the sanctuary.

Heaven still had mixed feelings, but she was just getting started. She wanted enough time for her perfume's invisible grasp to slay Averic. Her Clive Christian No. 1 perfume was the same scent she'd worn in Hawaii and throughout the brief time they'd stayed together. Her allure would depend upon both old and new tricks to get him back.

Everything came to a head on a rainy Friday night in June, when he changed the game she thought they'd been playing. "I love you like the air I breathe," he suddenly declared, "but I need to also be the man of God folks believe I am."

Averic downed the last bit of Jack Daniels straight from the bottle. One of the lies he'd tell her often was that it would never happen again. That night was different.

"I can't keep playing church. I want you to be there beside me. One day I'll have my own church. You'll make a perfect First Lady."

Despite him declaring how much he had grown to love her, deep inside she felt his proposal was so his conscience would stop its assault on his relationship with God.

Averic had never once asked Heaven how she felt about God becoming a priority in her life. Probably assumed that was a given because her father raised her in the church. He never asked if she'd wanted to become a First Lady, Second lady or Last lady of anyone's church, but by that night she had fallen in love with him too. Even more important, he'd always fervently made love to her the way she needed. His way was slow and sensually deliberate as if he'd created her body and knew every inch and nerve ending. Every time he reached a certain spot, he lingered, giving it "special attention." If he was God's gift to her, then she already loved his Lord because he was undoubtedly hearing her cries.

Facing Averic now, inside the sanctuary, Heaven relaxed her upper body slightly. She made a sudden sensual move against him that wouldn't allow him to escape the scent of freshly shampooed hair teasing his senses as those short curly tresses peppered his massive chest exposed at the top of his shirt. She was again amused when he staggered slightly, although he surely tried to control himself.

Heaven felt more powerful knowing Averic was probably now drunk with confusion for the moment. He could not, nor would he want to, escape the familiar warmth of her body. Her eyes remained shut as she enjoyed the tight embrace that took her back to a time and place with too many unresolved issues. Without a doubt, their bodies and minds had never stopped wanting or needing each other. She opened her eyes to find that tiny beads of sweat had suddenly appeared on his brow, as if reminding him of where they were.

They broke apart.

Pretending embarrassment, Heaven's head tilted slightly, this time like a cat uncertain if its prey was truly playing along or if it was just her imagination running away with her. Her eyes narrowed, observing Averic strain his neck to quickly scan the sanctuary, possibly looking for any church members or visitors. She allowed a small chuckle to escape because she knew, even if he didn't, they were still alone.

As he exhaled, her heart raced. She appreciated that the full color of his caramel complexion returned, erasing the red heat that had appeared seconds ago. Her face now betrayed nothing as she toyed with the idea of him pretending innocence, and not caring.

Heaven watched Averic allow his arms to swing slightly before clasping and shaking his hands several times; looking as though he wanted to shake whatever demon now controlled him.

"Are you okay?" Heaven asked with pretended concern. When she first left eighteen months ago, they'd kept in touch with a random phone call here and there. The last one helped her arrive at a place where she'd realized she couldn't go on without him. Heaven needed Averic. After all, he did preach forgiveness, and he said he'd forgiven her. Along with everything she wanted in her life, she also needed that.

"So, tell me something." Heaven's lips parted, slowly anticipating something savory about to happen, something she had not tasted in quite some time. She glanced at her watch before she spoke again. "Have you eaten?"

A sudden, but soft, stomach growl confirmed he was indeed

hungry. A simple question that his stomach answered before him, but she didn't press, knowing he might be embarrassed.

"I am starving--for something," she whispered.

"I'm embarrassed to say," he admitted, "but my stomach certainly thinks it needs substance."

Heaven found it quite funny that he couldn't seem to string two coherent words together.

"Well, I guess that's my answer," Heaven shot back as she slipped one of her arms through his. She began leading him out of the sanctuary. "I've only been in this part of Charleston a few times, but I've learned where the best restaurants are--and, of course, hotels."

"Hotels?"

"Of course, hotels," she mocked. "where did you think I was staying? You're the only family I have in Charleston."

* * *

AVERIC'S LIPS parted to speak, but it seemed that whatever words he wanted to say remained trapped.

Before Heaven arrived in Averic's life, he'd been a smart, savvy young man in his early thirties in the beginning stages of his charismatic ministry. He was the son of a well-known television preacher, Reverend Doctor Clyde Domingo. His father had prophesied shortly before his death that Averic would follow "mightily" in his footsteps. His father's signature message was, "There's nothing too hard for God. God forgives everything. Everything, except freaky nasty sexual things done to God's human temple whether by a heathen or by a child of God."

The congregation mostly had wholeheartedly agreed.

Averic had been respectful inside the church and out in the open, but sneaky in the dark. He had accepted his father's religious interpretation to a point, but he definitely didn't intend on being a virgin until a "holy woman" entered his life.

With his good looks and capitalizing upon his father's charismatic reputation, Averic made it his mission to prove his father wrong about keeping a Christian's sex life relegated to the missionary position. Hell, even missionaries went around the world. Averic spent a few years sampling the many beautiful honey pots where and when he could inside and outside the church.

A change finally came over Averic. An overzealous boyfriend of a lover didn't appreciate Averic consummating upon the same bed the boyfriend had slept in, and in the apartment the man had paid for.

That episode almost cost Averic his life. After leaving the hospital two weeks later with several well-healed stitches on the side of his face, he repented of his worldly escapades. He later accepted God's unmistakable call on his life as his father had prophesied.

Then Heaven came into his life.

He glanced at one of the red velvet-backed pews, then down at the plush red carpet, seemingly avoiding the wanton look in Heaven's topaz eyes. An unconscious wisp of air escaped his parted lips, signaling surrender to a desire he didn't want to feel.

Lord, give me strength.

The sound of the church's central air conditioner kicking on seemed louder than usual and startled Averic. He couldn't remember it doing that before and he felt a sudden chill, like someone was walking on his grave. Ignoring the most certain discernment in his spirit, he peered at her again.

She still had the ability to turn his world upside down just as she'd done that last night they'd spent in Honolulu. That night, with stars dotting the Hawaiian sky like glitter, she lay with him and was his personal luau. There was nothing left on her worldly menu that she didn't offer to satisfy his flesh.

Heaven had intimated that all they'd done over those last few days paled compared to what she was prepared to offer her Man of God. By the time she'd given her pre-show, including feats unimaginable to the most impressive double-jointed acrobat, Averic's entire body had turned into a combination of blue and anticipated ecstasy. She had hurt him so good without laying a hand on him.

No matter how much Averic had pleaded for her to end the feel-so-good sexual torture, she wouldn't. A long time had passed since she'd dropped the hint, laughing while she said she wanted a full commitment from him. For reasons he would never know, and without giving it much thought beyond his insatiable appetite for her, he'd proposed. He thought he'd sensed some hesitation because she'd stopped her usual laughter, but didn't immediately say yes. When she finally did respond, the answer barely passed her lips before he'd lifted her from the couch to the floor and celebrated the only way they truly knew.

"Heaven," he said, causing her to stop moving away from the pew. "This time, we need to be about more than the flesh. I love you still, and there's more to what I feel than--"

She parted her lips to protest, but he held up his hand.

"No, ma'am. We can't keep doing things the same way. I want my wife. All of her. Mind, body and soul."

* * *

AVERIC WAS unsure of the look on Heaven's face. Was it anger? Was it acceptance? He ran his fingers through his hair as though trying to pull more words from his head to make it clearer to her. He then laid that same hand over his heart. "I promise you, Heaven, I'll always love you. I hold you responsible for nothing."

He gestured to the papers he pulled from his pocket. "I'm supposed to be on a flight to a place where I'm talking to others about their marriages but looks like I need to be here to straighten out my own." Pointing to his stomach, he added. "And food can wait 'til later. Our present situation can't."

For a moment, Averic had considered giving in to his desires. He wanted Heaven so badly that he was in real pain from his waist to his knees. It had been eighteen months since they'd been man and wife. Now each month of separation was mocking him with what he'd been missing. But the pain he felt when she'd left him and the growth in his relationship with God, at that moment, gave him the strength and a reason to resist.

"You leaving me was a blessing and a curse," he said.

"Was it now?" Heaven's voice had a hint of sadness that he'd never heard before. "I'll just go."

She turned away.

"Not so fast," Averic told her. Gently touching her elbow, he turned her to face him, not allowing her feeble attempt at pulling away to dissuade him. "You'll leave when I finish saying what needs saying. But not here."

CHAPTER 5

*A*veric and Heaven had barely reached the sanctuary door to leave and engage in further discussion of their stalled marriage before Aunt Peaches came running inside. She glared, swinging a pocketbook and Bible like weapons, almost knocking Heaven aside. Without so much as an "excuse me" or even a glance toward Heaven, she began ranting.

"Averic, somebody done stole my battery out of my car! Who in the hell comes into a church parking lot on a Saturday afternoon in broad daylight and takes a battery from a car?"

He swung his head toward Heaven and shrugged. It was his way of apologizing for his aunt's obvious snub and disrespect for the sanctuary, despite what had occurred between them moments before. Nothing he could do about it because she was old and was blood.

She winked at him, assuring him that it was alright before turning toward Aunt Peaches to catch the rest of the old woman's familiar routine. Heaven knew drama, and young game recognized old game. A few more minutes passed while Heaven observed how Averic stood still with his arms folded and listened—or at least pretended to listen—to his aunt's promise to rain hellfire down on whoever stole her car battery.

Heaven laughed inside while almost feeling sorry for him. Aunt Peaches' mouth was still in overdrive as Averic gently maneuvered her by the arm out of the sanctuary and the church building with Heaven gliding right behind them.

"So, what can I do to help?" he asked as he guided his aunt toward the rear parking lot while beckoning with his free hand to Heaven, who had chosen to remain on the church steps.

"You can stop dragging me," Aunt Peaches barked. "I got bad knees and I can feel my heart racing."

She stopped fussing and abruptly turned toward Heaven, who had caught up to them before adding, "How you doing Heaven? I almost didn't recognize you since ain't nobody seen you since you up and broke my nephew's heart." Her eyes narrowed as she pointed at Heaven and continued, "God don't like ugly. He will kill it!"

"And yet you're still living," Heaven shot back, causing Averic to scowl. She hadn't meant to join Aunt Peaches' insinuating-mind game, but it was too late. Without a word of even an insincere apology, Heaven turned to Averic with the best fake smile she could muster. "Let's talk about things another time. I have to go back to my hotel room and my suitcases--"

"Oh, are you going away... perhaps forever?" Aunt Peaches asked, sounding a lot less like a question, and more like hope.

"Traveling mercies then—for the other travelers," Aunt Peaches added. Without giving Averic a chance to say so much as a goodbye to Heaven, she yanked him by the arm and angled him toward the parking lot. She did it without any sign of a bad knee or heart.

He always marveled at how his late uncle Bud had put up with her busybody ways for thirty years before he'd decided to just catch pneumonia and die. No one could convince Averic his uncle hadn't gotten sick on purpose, because Uncle Bud would have been crazy to stay outside most of the night in the backyard naked and in the freezing rain.

"Should've left your crazy aunt at that daggone Shack Bar in Columbia where I met her," he'd often complain before he passed away. "Should've listened when she told me her love was free, but it was gonna cost me a plenty!"

Uncle Bud wasn't crazy, just hen-pecked to death. Now it looked like Aunt Peaches aimed for Averic to join him in glory.

He caught a glimpse of Heaven's back as she scampered away with her high heels clicking rapidly on the pavement, sounding like gunshots. His heart quickened. He was certain that she wanted to be with him and not just for what he could do in bed. What other reason was there for her to come? He had to establish how things were to be. No more little thinking. He needed to think big. Starting right then.

"Was that necessary?" he barked. "That's my wife. I've forgiven her, and besides, one day you may have to witness to Heaven about Jesus."

"No, I won't."

"You won't?" he asked, stopping abruptly. His aunt didn't care much for Heaven. She never had, but he didn't expect such an un-Christian-like response.

"I ain't got to talk to Heaven about Jesus cause that heffa's going straight to Hell!"

Averic exhaled. Discussing it any further was a waste of time because now he had another question.

"Heaven," he yelled right before she made it to her car.

She turned, and his lengthy silence carried his meaning as she slowly made her way back to where they stood.

"Aunt Peaches ..." He dropped her arm and scanning the empty parking lot. "where's your car?"

An innocent expression spread over her chubby face. Her creamy complexion turned bright red as she lit up like a child opening a gift on Christmas morning. "My car's at home."

"You *lied?*"

"Not exactly. I did come by *car* today." She shrugged. "I took an Uber."

Averic could feel the anger building up, erasing any of the good feeling left when Heaven showed up unexpectedly. "What the Hell is wrong with you?"

Heaven's eyebrow winged upward as she tried to hold in a smirk.

"It's a good thing we ain't inside the House of God, 'cause you ain't acting like no preacher right now," Aunt Peaches snapped. The color drained from her face and her brow furrowed. "I just saved you a world of pain. Who did you come crying to when that piece of trash left you?"

"I wasn't crying."

"I saw a tear."

"One tear," he shot.

"Where there's one, there's more."

Heaven's face flamed a bright red, and she blinked three times before she put her focus on Averic.

Aunt Peaches continued, reminding Averic of how far he'd come since he accepted that Heaven had abandoned him, ending with, "I told you back then, you don't pick fruit out of season and expect it to be ripe and good for you unless you planning on canning it or getting poisoned." With a dismissive wave at Heaven, she commanded, "You need to let it go. Let her go."

"Aunt Peaches." Averic felt like pulling his ears from his head if it would keep him from hearing her nag. "I appreciate all you did for me when I needed a listening ear."

"That's right," Aunt Peaches snarled. "You didn't call on Jesus that night when she left and took everything, leaving you nothing but your Michael Jord drawers. That heffa didn't even leave the A and the N when she took them."

Heaven flinched but remained silent.

Aunt Peaches had stung him good with her inference that Heaven had left him without a pot to piss in and his favorite underwear. But Averic was in no mood to quibble over drawers.

"Well, I'm calling on Him now," he snapped, "because if I don't, I will say something I cannot take back. She-is-my-life."

Aunt Peaches gasped at hearing those words. So did Heaven.

"What you mean? Your *life*?" she asked, her lips trembling. "I thought Jesus was your life."

"Heaven is *still* my wife," he corrected, kicking himself for that slip.

"And you don't get to talk to her, or about her, like that. You don't do it at all. Do you understand?"

Silence.

Heaven folded her arms over her ample bosom.

Aunt Peaches' lips parted as though she wanted to speak, then clamped shut as she smiled. "Well, good for you," she snapped as a twinkle replaced the evil stare she'd given Averic. "It's about time you stood up for her. How did you expect me or anybody to respect her if you don't ever act like you respect her?"

Averic threw his arms in the air, glaring at his aunt.

"Jesus," he cried out. "this woman!"

He had finally reached the point where he realized how much he loved his wife. All it took was his crazy old aunt to get him to say and do something he should have done months ago.

"No matter what I said or didn't say," he countered, "you had no reason or cause to speak to Heaven or anyone like that. You're supposed to be winning souls, not scaring them away."

She shook her fleshy fist at him. "Averic, please. I used to change your pissy diapers. I earned that right the hard way."

Heaven averted her gaze, trying not to laugh.

Aunt Peaches smiled then ignored his anger before changing the subject. "We can pray about my bad Christian behavior and your cowardice while you drive me home."

"Yes," Averic replied. "We need prayer." He shifted his gaze to Heaven. "Call me in fifteen minutes to make sure I'm still alive or that I don't need bail money."

Heaven chuckled and sashayed toward the other side of the parking lot.

One moment Averic had Heaven by the arm and the possibility of the woman he loved in his life again. Now old Hell was dragging him toward his car.

Life just got more complicated.

CHAPTER 6

"She said *what*?" Heaven was laughing so hard she had to pull her cell away from her ear and sit down. She could barely catch her breath. She had reached out to Averic at the very moment he was leaving his Aunt Peaches' home.

"What Aunt Peaches said didn't bother me that much," Averic said, joining in the laughter. "She'll always be Aunt Peaches. Fresh or canned."

"That's true," Heaven agreed. Her voice became suddenly softer, though serious. "But on another note, I'll only be in Charleston for another week. I'm on a vacation of sorts, but I do have a job interview this Friday that may change my plans."

"What are your plans until then?"

"My invitation to dine still stands if you're as hungry as I am," she teased. "Your stomach is probably already at the nearest restaurant waiting for you to catch up."

* * *

THIRTY MINUTES LATER, Averic knocked on Heaven's door on the seventh floor of the Charleston Cathedral Hotel. As soon as it opened, the scent of her intoxicating perfume hit like a hammer upside his head. Oddly, he could never remember its name, but he did remember how much he loved watching her walk, and she did not disappoint today. She wore a neon blue cotton skirt with her signature slit almost to the waist. Every time she moved, that slit moved the opposite way. Averic smiled. *She even knows how to train her clothes to be sexy.*

"Thanks again for not holding Aunt Peaches' bad behavior against me," he said as he followed her further into the room. The place was nothing like the hotel room where he imagined Heaven would stay. The room was painted beige with a stucco design inlay. One king-sized bed, table, and table lamp. A combo television with a radio playing soft music on a swivel stand cabinet occupied the far corner. The usual mini-bar below the television and off to the side was a few feet away from a reasonably sized bathroom with a double sink. Two large suitcases were crammed into a far corner. Although it wasn't the type of hotel rooms they'd shared in the past, it was still expensive. Heaven could spend the maximum even when she got the minimum.

After offering Averic a spot on the small love seat near the cathedral window, Heaven pulled the cord on the window's white curtains to allow a bit of sunlight into the room.

"So, like I said, I'll be here for the upcoming week," she informed him. Heaven came over and sat close enough for a knee to almost touch his before continuing. "I know it's sudden, but other than tonight what are your plans, if I may ask?"

The question caught him off guard. With Heaven, he could never be sure if a question was just a question or the beginning of a real interrogation.

"I sent a text to the conference organizers letting them know I'd be flying out tomorrow instead of today," he replied. Without thinking, he added, "It's more important to be with you."

She blinked, but he could see the tears welling in her eyes. "Where is it?"

"In Hawaii."

Heaven pushed away and leaned on the back of the love seat. "Hawaii? You're kidding me. Right?"

He tried to pretend he didn't see the relevance or react to what might have been either pleasurable or painful to her. "It was no big deal. Instead of me speaking toward the beginning of the conference, I asked to trade places with someone else and speak toward the end," he explained. He flexed a finger between the two of them. "This right here is my emergency and I plan on handling it right now."

* * *

"Welcome to Honolulu," a husky male voice announced over the loudspeaker from inside the plane's cockpit.

Hours earlier, Averic had taken a protesting Heaven by her arm with one hand and snatched one of the large suitcases with his other, then checked her out of the hotel.

"Whatever you need I'll buy when we get to Hawaii," he'd promised while they engaged in a tug of war on the elevator ride down.

She'd fussed all the way to the Charleston airport. Once inside the terminal, she'd come close to having airport security arrest him for kidnapping while he exchanged his plane ticket and purchased a round trip for her.

"For the last time, Averic," she had argued loudly which had caused security to take notice. "You can't just up and make me go somewhere with you. I told you I have a job interview. I don't know who in the Hell you think you are."

He'd laughed, then with an exaggerated sweeping motion with one hand, he turned to the concerned onlookers and blurted, "How many of you ladies would love for your man to whisk you away to a romantic island on a moment's notice?"

From the crowd, female hands shot up like he'd announced, "This is a robbery. Put 'em up." Several jealous females glared at their men, but security just gave him a high-five approval as they walked away laughing.

Heaven hadn't seen that extreme side of him before. Observing how the other women reacted to his assertiveness had made her realize it was one of the manly ingredients she'd needed and missed in their marriage. Within moments she'd felt that she no longer had to lead him as well as follow. She wasn't certain how long that change would last, but her curiosity was at an all-time high, and she'd calmed down as they'd boarded their flight.

Taking no chances, she sat in the aisle seat just in case she was wrong. Heaven needed the extra space to rain down hell upon him if he'd misled her.

Heaven glanced over at Averic. Evidently, the good pastor had forgotten what he'd said to her the last time she was able to get him on the phone.

"I had to accept your decision to leave," he declared. *"I'd already promised I was giving my life, that time, totally over to God. Perhaps you were an experience I needed to go through."*

How could she ever forget? She learned from that one phone conversation that she'd been reduced to just a wife after falling completely in love, willing to sacrifice it all so her husband could be completely and spiritually involved in his ministry. But all she'd been was an "experience."

But he seemed to be saying something different back at the hotel. He wanted a full-time wife instead? He wanted her? First lady? Was that all? He didn't want her the way she wanted. The thought tied her in knots.

As far as her relationship with God stood, Heaven still wasn't sure of her footing. Although her father had been a bishop and her husband now a true Man of God, it didn't mean she felt secure in her faith.

If her prayers meant anything in Paradise, then God would not interfere. Didn't the Bible say, 'Whosoever God put together, let no man put asunder?' Why wouldn't her prayers be just as important to God as was Averic? After all, she had not slept around on Averic the entire time they'd been apart when she definitely could have. That must count for something. Why hadn't she considered it before?

Being that close to her husband for the long flight, she realized that maybe she was wrong. She also realized that she needed to keep him in her life, even if only as a friend. If he allowed even that much.

That was nine hours ago.

Whatever problems they had as man and wife had brought them to this place of understanding. They needed a marriage renovation. Perhaps it would finally take place now that they were in a different seventh-floor hotel room in Hawaii.

"THERE'S something you might have missed about me the other day in the sanctuary." His voice deepened as he pointed to the sofa. "Please. Just sit down a moment."

Heaven moved slowly, continuing to look over her shoulder at Averic as she made her way to take a seat. Her apprehension was apparent when she took a few seconds longer than necessary to sit.

"It's no secret you weren't high on the congregation's First Lady list. They made that clear when most didn't vote to make me co-pastor right after we were married."

Heaven's eyes narrowed as her mouth opened to speak. "I lost count of how many times you said you didn't care about that. I felt so … unworthy."

"What was I supposed to say?" he asked. "You were my wife. Was I supposed to kick you out of my life because a few acted like they'd not ever committed a sin? You were as worthy as the others. I know that *now* for a fact."

AVERIC STOPPED SUDDENLY in the middle of the same argument he'd tried to make since they'd arrived. It took him a moment to realize she hadn't interrupted that time. No need. Her tears spoke instead. Droplets escaped down Heaven's cheek, leaving a mascara path. Her pained expression tugged at him. He would not stop. He could not stop. Too much was at stake. They may have slid into this backwards

—almost breech—but there was time and a way to straighten things out.

"What I've been trying to get you to understand is that shortly after you left, the congregation put my name on the ballot to take Pastor Mark's place when he retires in a few weeks. And whether they like it or not, I intend to have my wife--*my* First Lady by my side. I don't care what they say or how they feel about it."

Averic watched as Heaven turned her head, sniffing softly trying to hold back the rest of tears. He knew her well enough to see it was her foolish pride still trying to interfere, but her sad eyes betrayed her. No doubt in his mind she'd heard every word. His words were the surgical knife cutting away the doubt that he was indeed the man. He was the whole man and husband with no chance of going back to what was.

Heaven suddenly slithered toward the window and closed the curtains. She sauntered over to where Averic remained seated and slowly unwrapped her skirt, pulling it apart from the bottom of its slit.

Averic watched her closely as the scent of her perfume sought him out for a sensual attack. She still thought this was all about her body.

He leaned back against the sofa as though she'd mysteriously muted him. He then remembered how he'd nearly given in the first night after they arrived. Cold showers hadn't helped much. He'd prayed half-heartedly that night for restraint before finally sleeping on the hotel room sofa, which had given some relief, but not much.

"A wife is supposed to feed her husband," Heaven began, and her tone had an innocence about it. She opened the slit of her skirt, and he hit the brakes with a sudden sprint across the room to reopen the curtains. "I know what you're doing, Heaven, and it still won't work."

She might have heard the caution in his words, but the outlined imprint in his pants showed something hugely different. He couldn't control his body's response to his wife, but he could control how he acted on things.

"What's the problem?" There was real hurt in her question; she didn't try to hide it that time. She took a deep breath. "I'm your wife. You're my husband."

"I want to get to know my wife," he said. "I need to know you entirely. In my awkward way, I keep trying to explain that to you. We've got the sex part of things down pat. What about the other parts of us?"

Heaven lifted her head high like a queen, closing the slit in her skirt as though it were an accident that it had opened.

"There's so much more I want to tell you," Averic confessed while pulling Heaven closer, then gently putting a little distance between them as though she were fragile. "I played at church, and I certainly played at being a husband--"

Averic sensed her attention beginning to wane. "The reason I consented to being a speaker at this conference was to share an experience many Men of God go through."

"What are you talking about?" Heaven asked, relaxing as he touched her elbow. Something she said always soothed her.

"I'm not the first man or the last who preaches one thing about sex and does something else. Every time I touched you, especially after we married, the guilt still consumed me."

Heaven's mouth gaped. *Is he crazy or having a breakdown?* Her comfort from his touch faded as she tried pulling away.

"You don't have to be afraid of me," Averic said, reaching for her and stroking the side of her face; a move he'd used often to calm her and show how much he cared. He wasn't sure if it would work at that moment, but he tried anyway. "Touching you in ways that the world would consider freaky and some might even say unnatural was against everything I taught, embraced, and preached. Yet, you allowing me to do those things and seeing how much pleasure it brought you made me feel more of a man than I ever had."

Her eyes sparkled when he added, "And don't think I didn't enjoy it. The enjoyment was what made me feel overwhelmed with guilt. How could I tell others not to do what we were doing--when I was laid up with you, Heaven? Even though we were married--woman, you were putting me through Hell, and I liked it!"

He suddenly kissed her forehead.

Her brow furrowed slightly, showing even more of her confusion. "Are you wanting a divorce?" she asked. "What is it that you're trying to tell me? Can you get to the point, please? What does any of this have to do with a conference?"

Averic smiled, seeing her confusion dissolving into anger. So, *she* was supposed to keep the upper hand. *He* was supposed to want her back without preconditions not travel down memory lane in Hawaii. Not happening.

"Heaven, I went into therapy."

"For what?" she snapped. "Hypocrisy?"

"I guess you could call it that. I--finally read the Bible."

"You hadn't read it before?" she asked, her eyes narrowing with suspicion. "How could you preach and say you'd not read your Bible? Even *I* know better than that, and I'm far from anybody's Bible scholar."

"I finally read it and the Song of Solomon too, this time with understanding along with spiritual guidance."

"I hope you get to the point quicker at your conference than you are now," Heaven countered. "You're not making a bit of sense and I'm getting tired."

"I've been speaking about this part of marriage for the last six months."

Heaven pulled away so fast she could have broken Averic's arm. "Speaking about *our* marriage? You got a lot of nerve! You can speak about it with a bunch of strangers, but you couldn't reach out to me."

Averic threw up his hands in surrender, muttered something unintelligible, and started for the door to escape into the hallway. Before he reached it, he turned back. "I've been speaking on Hebrews 13:4."

"You know I don't know one Hebrew from another," she shot back. "What in the world does that have to do with you putting our marriage on blast at some doggone conferences?"

Averic hadn't meant to take it any further. Before he knew it, he'd turned and was headed toward Heaven with words leaving his mouth like an Uzi shooting bullets. "Hebrews 13:4," he shot, almost coming toe-to-toe with his wife. "Marriage is honorable in 'all,' and the bed-undefiled; but whoremongers and adulterers God will judge."

"Are you calling me a whore?" Heaven's words were laced with spit and anger.

"Hell, no," Averic blurted. "Did you not just hear what I said?"

"You said I was a whore and an adulterer and God was gonna judge me. I haven't slept with anyone, real or imagined, since I've been with you. You don't get to call me a whore."

"You heard what you wanted to hear." Averic put his hands on his waist to keep them from putting them where they didn't need to go—a good slap on her backside. "I said the marriage bed is undefiled. The *marriage bed* is undefiled."

He felt the heat racing from his head and down his face. His blood pressure rose at a fast pace, but he would have his say if it killed him. "You need to know, like I've been trying to tell you for the past thirty-six hours, that I realize guilt has no place here. I will be a complete husband, and you need to stop playing head games."

"Say what?" Heaven's tiny hands warped into big fists. *This fool is crazy!*

"You are more to me than a sexy body," Averic ranted. "You will get old and saggy--"

Heaven hissed through clenched teeth, pointing to her large breasts. "These two Scud missiles are all muscles, baby. They ain't never gonna sag. You can take that to the bank."

"I've changed my mind," Averic said with a sigh.

* * *

HIS RESPONSE WASN'T what Heaven had expected. He was swinging her mind like a pendulum, and that wasn't sitting well with her. Had she made a mistake in returning?

"About what?"

"In fact," Averic continued as if he hadn't heard her speak. As if on cue, the radio that they'd set on auto when they'd first arrived began playing. He walked to the nightstand and turned the knob. "Let's turn this thing down. You need to hear me loud and clear. I'm not leaving tomorrow after the conference."

She hoped by the way he was moving that he was now as deeply committed to making their marriage work, as she needed to be. He'd slept on the couch, took cold showers—twice a day—and spent that time asking questions about her life, her past, and what she wanted to do in life. He listened. Truly listened.

Heaven wanted to remain indifferent, but she failed. "You're not leaving? Why not?"

Averic paced the length of the room. "How can I come here and tell someone what to do in their life and marriage and leave with so much left undone in my own?" His face turned into a mask of contrition set in a firm foundation of truth. "I can't do it," he whispered.

Heaven hoped she didn't imagine Averic's confession.

Like night and day, Averic suddenly smiled. "We're not going anywhere."

"We're not?"

He stopped pacing and walked swiftly to her side. She didn't back away. She scanned Averic's face for further truths, but his next move confused her further. He kissed her. His lips traveled along her cheek, taking tongue laps from one ear across to the other.

"I love you, Mrs. Heaven Foxx Domingo," he whispered. "I thank God for you."

Heaven absorbed the beauty of those words and whispered, "I'm willing to try."

Averic moved in to hold her. "That's all I ask. Meet me halfway."

CHAPTER 7

Heaven's heart raced as she extracted herself from his hold and gave him a sideways look. Could she believe him? Should she believe he loved her--for her? His declaration made Heaven want to testify. He had put everything on hold to save their marriage. She felt like running around that hotel room like she'd seen church folk do at revivals, but the only place she wanted to run to at that moment was further into Averic's arms. She felt a part of his entire being. Her ark of safety was right where she stood.

Three days later, Heaven awakened in Averic's arms as she had for the past three mornings of the conference, which ended yesterday. They opted to stay another few days to rekindle the more positive parts of the marriage. Walking on the beach, touring the island, sharing their innermost thoughts, and working through their issues one by one.

And on the seventh day of her return, Heaven had an epiphany. "I've decided something," she said. "No more cold showers for us, ever again," she whispered as she slid from under the covers and headed toward the bathroom. "I will always want my husband in all the ways a husband should be."

"You'll get no argument from me." Averic teased before he added. "I want you, too. And I'm glad we've come to an understanding."

"Understanding is an understatement," Heaven shouted over the sound of water running in the shower. "If I wasn't sure I'd break the glass in this shower door I'd sing like Minnie Ripperton did when she sang 'Loving You'."

Averic shouted, "Stick to what you know," from the other room causing Heaven to laugh and swallow some of the hot shower water. "Give me a minute to refresh my memory," she coughed.

Minutes later, inside the Romanesque-styled double sink bathroom, she called out to Averic to join her.

"Is it hot in here to you?" Heaven grabbed a large bath towel. She patted her wet hair that had formed short ringlets. The harder she patted, the more she looked like the cartoon character, Betty Boop.

Averic gently pulled the towel from her hands. "Come here, wife." At the rate you're patting that gorgeous head of hair you're gonna be bald--hmm," he began smiling, "I've never been a big fan of the Grace Jones look, but it just might work on you."

"Yeah right," she teased. "Me and Grace Jones got only one thing in common."

"What's that?"

Heaven pulled the towel from Averic's hand. She began wrapping it around her waist as she sang, *"Pull up to the bumper, ba-a-by."*

* * *

NOT WANTING to disappoint or deny his wife's request, Averic snatched the towel away without giving another thought to any semblance of a Grace Jones look or any other look. Slowly turning her around, he moved her so that she couldn't move away from the sink and began *polishing* the hood, the dashboard, the headlights, and her bumper just the way he knew she'd want.

By the time he finished the second time, she was singing Nelly Travis's "If I Back It Up Whatchu' Gonna Do?"

A short time later, Heaven began massaging his sweaty muscles as though she wanted them to embrace her again. "I keep thinking about the Hebrews scripture we talked about. The more I think about it, the more I'm certain I'm going to mess up a little, probably a lot—"

"That makes two of us. That's what grace and mercy are all about." Averic replied softly as he closed his eyes and whispered, "Thank God."

Kicking the sheets aside, she reached over a few inches for the glass of water on the nightstand. Between sipping the cold liquid, she confessed. "I'm not going to be the perfect First Lady. My faith is a little shaky."

"Everybody's working, struggling with faith." Averic took the glass from her hand and took a sip of his own before placing on the nightstand on his side of the bed. "Just know that we'll work on ours together."

"Thank you for not giving up on me." *Thank you, Jesus, for hanging with me too.*

As if he'd read her thoughts, Averic smiled. "God gave me the right woman as my wife. Took me on a detour to get her, but Heaven is mine."

***

HEAVEN SMILED, "I'm one hundred percent yours 'cause ninety-nine-and-a-half just won't do." She blew him a kiss without waiting for him to respond and looked down at her husband. Pointing, with one finger. "The cuffs and keys are in that top drawer under the television."

Averic grinned and swung his head in the direction of the dresser, then narrowed his gaze on her. "You already knew? Do you keep them in your pocketbook?" He laughed aloud before he blew a kiss at her. "They've been there the whole time, haven't they?"

"What made you think that?" she asked with a wink.

"Outsmarted again." Averic went for the handcuffs and turned up the radio.

"Remember this move?" he asked, beginning a slow strip tease as he unbuttoned his shirt. He exposed muscles fit for the feast laying before him and let his pants drop to the floor. He picked his clothes up, winked at her, and looked down. His gaze stopped at his mid-thigh before he looked at her again.

"I could probably hang these right on this," he teased, pointing to the throbbing muscle he knew she really wanted, and he wanted to give her. "But I'll just toss them on the bed instead."

The sexual anticipation in the room was thick enough to make a California fog look clear. Heaven quickly fished two pillows from the bed and lay down next to him on the floor with one of the pillows under her head. "You ain't the only one who knows how to pray."

We serve an amazing God.

Averic had just placed one end of the handcuffs around one of Heaven's small wrists with the other end around one of the nightstand legs when he spied the pillows.

"Pillows. That's so thoughtful, baby." He smiled as he reached for one.

Heaven stopped him with her free hand. "That's not for you."

"No?"

"No," she teased while placing the extra pillow under her hips. They're both for me."

She shimmied on the pillow until she felt she was in the right position. "You said something when we first met about me being an appetizer."

"I remember that," he replied, laughing. "And I plan on having you a la carte for the rest of our lives."

"Well, I'll adjust myself on this pillow-tray; there's so much of me to sample."

Averic lowered himself to the floor.

For hours, Heaven and Averic continued their reunion foreplay. Every time they caught their breath, they'd start rejuvenating again with tales of spicy adventures, each trying to outdo the other with various innovative ways of recalling the events.

"You remember that time when I had a menu typed up detailing a full course selection of intercourse du jour?" Heaven teased.

"I remember that the only attire I had to wear was a tie."

"And, you wore it so well," Heaven added with a chuckle.

"Oh please," Averic teased. "Don't you ever forget how you loved wearing those cherry-flavored edible panties that night on a hot beach in Maui and they melted."

"That's true," Heaven replied, feigning embarrassment, and placing a hand over her heart. "But they didn't go to waste, did they?"

"Sure didn't," Averic responded, licking his fingers. "It was one tasty night."

"And remember when we had to pay for that glass-topped table at the Polynesian Cultural Center?" She stood and waved a finger at Averic. "You were just nasty."

"How was I nasty?" Averic asked as he rose and towered over her. "Tell me that. How was making love to my wife nasty? It was your idea to spice things up and get on top of that glass table in the first place."

"I can show you better than I can tell you, Reverend Averic Domingo," Heaven taunted. She turned and opened the drawer above the mini bar. Pulling out a small bottle of orange liquid, she laughed and continued. "You do remember this, don't you, Mr. Nasty?"

He took the bottle from her hand, turning it over in his large hands, and burst out laughing. "Licking Lotion."

He shook his head. "Tangerine-flavored."

"And you will have a fantastic full course meal, 'cause you've got me on your menu." She gave him a quick wink. "You can't deny we were deliciously made for each other."

Averic returned her wink with one of his. "Testify woman. You are rib of my rib."

Heaven tenderly pulled Averic toward her. Her eyes swept over him, telegraphing all that was unnecessary to say in her heart. "Well then, let's get this sexy barbeque started while the coals are hot."

They'd barely begun to sample again from the marriage menu when suddenly the radio's song choice switched from the O'Jays' "Forever Mine" to "Climbing the Stairway to Heaven."

* * *

Thank you for reading *Heaven Can Hell*. I wanted to show what could happen when a confident, carnal-minded woman works her magic to seduce a sexually inhibited reverend. She got him but now can she keep him if God wants him too, kinky-free? It answers the question ... is the bed ever defiled between a consenting husband and wife when their explorations go outside the regular "missionary" position.

Please leave a review, it would be much appreciated.

Check out what's coming March 20, 2019

FIRE IN THE WATER

Celeste Francois

Unlike the pigeons that happily pecked at crumbs on the dirty sidewalk below her apartment, Brooklyn's own unlucky pigeon, Celeste Francois, felt like a hostage. For several years, she'd been tied and strangled by the ropes of poverty. She'd given in to believing she'd never leave that New York borough and become a dove.

She'd been awake since the sun came on duty earlier, still lying across her full-size bed, summoning all her overweight ancestors to come to her aid.

While the weather outside was warm and welcoming, inside Celeste Francois' tiny apartment, a storm was brewing.

"I am more than a conqueror," she told herself. Unfortunately, no amount of self-convincing or hypnotism in the world could handle all her belly fat. She found ways to camouflage it over the past nine years, off and on, by wearing the latest late-night 'Get-Skinny-Quick' gimmick that never worked. Her daily routine consisted of trying to cram her pounds of all the post-pregnancy fat into a pair of plus size jeans.

"This don't make no doggone sense," she pined, groaning with all the effort. "I just bought these a month ago." She rolled her eyes to the ceiling while thinking of a million other things she'd rather do on her thirty-fifth birthday.

"Mama, please hurry. We're hungry."

The plea came from her ten-year-old identical twins, Jeanette, and Jonnay, her mini-me opinionated girls. When they weren't working her nerves, she did everything to spoil them. She had very little but was filled with determination to give the pair of energetic, coffee-colored, four foot ninety pounds of pig-tailed, dawn-to-evening questioning kids, the love and attention she'd never received.

Looking away from Celeste, the twins twisted their lips trying to hide the sneer they knew might bring them closer to a threat of a spanking than they'd want.

Under her steely gaze, they swallowed their comments but glanced at each other. With complaints silently shared—a twin-thing they'd learned at a young age—they continued struggling to balance a huge box between them.

Though the twins had remained silent, tt didn't stop Celeste from ranting as though she'd read their minds. "Will you two just stop aggravating me?" Celeste snapped. Sweat popped from her forehead as she motioned to herself. "You two see I'm trying to get dressed."

Jeannette, a bit older than her twin by almost three minutes, replied dryly, "Ain't nobody trying to aggravate you, Mama. One of them moving men say they done you a favor even coming here yesterday, and today. He said he's gonna just put the rest of your 'crappy' stuff back on the truck." She took a deep breath. "He say he's gonna drive off if you don't pay them the rest of they money."

Jeanette quickly lifted her chin and nodded at her twin. "Didn't he say that, Jonnay?"

Jonnay, following her sister's lead as always, sighed. "He sure did." Jonnay's hands jerked as she shifted her end of the box, filled to the top with her mama's good dishes. "And I'm getting tired."

Celeste moaned, and stared at the ceiling. She grimaced, and then set her face in a determined mask despite the pain.

Maybe it was tiredness that made Jonnay forget her second-place status. She went full rogue and wasn't through complaining.

"That other man," she began, "the one smelling like a skunk wearing bad vanilla—like you always say when somebody is stinking—said that 'cause you went out a time or two wasn't enough reason to let you slide on the rest, Mama." She sped up to get the rest of her report out. "He was even winking like something was in his eyes when he said to tell you that. And then he said, real loud, like he wanted everybody outside to hear, that y'all can discuss it like yawl used to." She hunched her shoulders adding, "Whatever that means."

"Yeah, but—" Jeanette chimed in. "That other man with those black ashy ears like a homeless bunny rabbit said there wasn't gonna be no discussion. Just pay him his—" she frowned. "He said a bad word—money."

Defeated, Celeste dropped her head to her chin. Struggling, Celeste threw her head back onto the pillow. "C'mon now." She gritted her teeth. Her hips bobbed like two overripe cantaloupes with stretch marks. "Finally," she announced as the jeans made its way to her waist without getting anything caught in its zipper.

Celeste slid off the side of the bed and didn't so much as blink. She gestured with a flip of one hand, ordering, "Pick up that box." Then, she slipped into a pair of house shoes that once had two-inch heels. Over time, her weight had turned them into a pair of no-inch flats. "Lay it in the corner next to the refrigerator."

Jonnay scanned the room, then looked at her sister as though waiting for Jeanette's approval to speak. Her brown eyes narrowed as she inquired, "Mama, where's the rest of the kitchen? When we got here last night, I thought it was bigger."

"Yeah , mama," Jeanette, added. "The last three places we lived we didn't have to walk out of it and turn around to get to the stove." She tossed the question to her sister. "Ain't that right, Jonnay?"

Jonnay nodded. "Didn't have to think about opening the fridge first to get inside the oven or the other way round, too."

Celeste frowned at the girls, resting her hands on her massive hips.

Her head swung between them, giving each the old Southern Mama's 'evil eye'.

The girls gulped and swallowed whatever words were on the tip of their tongues as they trotted away to do as they were ordered.

Celeste hung her head, whispering a prayer. "Lord, how long do I have to live like this? Can I at least catch a break on my birthday?" Not waiting for an answer, or truly expecting one, she opened the door and waddled down to the steps from her one-bedroom, third-floor walk-up apartment.

"Those girls deserve better than this," she whispered. "It doesn't make no sense I need to keep moving because I don't always have the rent." Winded, she stopped and rested against a wooden bannister for a moment.

Two flights down to go and two angry men; one wanting money, the other want "something" more. Celeste simply wanted some peace of mind and a better life for her girls. And, if life would finally be so kind, she'd also like to get her hands around Sanjay Thomas' neck and send him to meet his maker.

Sanjay Thomas

Many New York residents struggled to survive, but not in Sanjay Thomas's world. Life was getting better everyday in almost every way. Except two things—Al Green's famous love and happiness.

Inside his spacious five-bedroom, three-and-a-half bath home—complete with manicured grounds and a huge two-car garage situated in the posh area of Westchester County, New York—he whispered, "God, thank you for being the God of second chances."

Sanjay shook his head, as he'd done often, at how far he'd come in the past year alone. The smooth sounds of Richard Smallwood's 'Angels Watching Over Me' echoed from the Bose system. He scooted back onto his sofa and gave an audible sigh while scanning his surroundings. His lavish ivory-and-taupe living room was equipped with Cathedral windows that stood open to let in the cool night air.

He leaped off the sofa, clasping his fingers together and forming a temple before dropping his head. In submission, he stood before a large, expensive oil painting of Jesus. The picture hung above a white, marbled fireplace overlooking several awards for his gold and platinum gospel compositions displayed across its mantle. Sanjay's broad shoulders swayed as thoughts that wavered between gratefulness and loneliness nearly overwhelmed him. After all, with so many blessings raining down on him, a forty-something year-old man shouldn't cry. Besides, a pair of bloodshot and puffy eyes wouldn't look good on the cover of Today's Inside Gospel magazine.

Finally, looking up and exhaling, Sanjay checked his two-thousand-dollar IWC Portugieser Automatic watch with its legendary Pellaton winding system and ceramic components. *Father God, I'm still conflicted. Perhaps I shouldn't have accepted such an extravagant gift from the Board of Bishops.*

Yet he had, especially when the board explained, "You've put our congregation on the map. Every concert, conference, or play we've produced over the past fifteen months has been phenomenal and financially successful. And if we preach prosperity, then our ministry needs to look prosperous. You're going to be on the cover of a famous gospel magazine. You can't be wearing some cheap, on-sale watch from Amazon."

Would the Board feel that way if they knew the truth about him? That question haunted Sanjay because they didn't know his entire testimony. Sanjay had wanted to tell them on so many occasions. He'd wanted to confess how his past wasn't always pretty. Once he overcame homelessness and other pitfalls of life, he didn't want to remember any of those ugly experience. Every success stabbed his conscience despite the words of gratitude that spewed off his tongue. Sanjay was convinced God would place him in a situation where he'd have no choice but to tell it all. "Thank you, Lord, for new mercies every day," he whispered.

So far, he hadn't been exposed, but that didn't stop him from looking over his shoulder while holding a glimmer of faith.

Twenty minutes later, after the news van arrived, the camera crew snapped pictures of him in various poses around the living room. Thankfully, the interview didn't take long. The female journalist, who wore a form-fitting dress that left nothing to anyone's imagination, asked the same questions as all the other entertainment papers. When she kept smoothing her dress or pursing her lips when she spoke. Sanjay instantly picked up that she was a bit more flirty than professional. Also apparent, was the fact that his now burgeoning size didn't matter. He had the three "F"s some women liked ... Fame, Fortune, and Flash.

He'd smiled and played it safe by giving her details of his obligatory made-up past. Sanjay scattered in enough distorted facts to blame the magazine if his answers proved false or his past was discovered. As hard as he'd prayed for forgiveness, his pride always interfered. Either way, he never revealed his complete history to anyone.

"I can't thank you enough for this wonderful opportunity and blessing," Sanjay smiled at the attractive columnist from Today's Inside Gospel magazine as he escorted her and the crew outside. "It didn't take too long for you to get me to spill everything," he teased, knowing she'd been able to do anything but.

"You were an excellent interviewee," she replied, running a hand through her silky weave for the umpteenth. "Can I call you directly if I need any further info?"

"I certainly hope I've given you all you need." Sanjay spoke slowly, hoping she understood there wouldn't be a follow up. Just in case he wasn't clear, he added, "I'm about to go back into my creative cave and write. It's how I stay on top. I hope you understand."

If she understood, she said nothing. Pushing one of the crew aside, she hurried inside the van but not before glaring over her shoulder at Sanjay. Then, a false smile appeared on her ruby-red lips when she looked at him again. A shiver of unease slithered up his spine.

Back inside his home, Sanjay pondered what had just gone down and the real or perceived threat of being discovered by the female reporter who hadn't accepted 'not interested' as an answer.

Sure, he was riding high now, yet eleven years ago he couldn't have caught a ride in a three-wheeled shopping cart. Back then he had two patched shirts, two pairs of dark-colored pants, and a pair of shoes that had seen the inside of an old shoe repair shop more than the shop's resident roaches.

Things hadn't always been that way. The year before he'd joined the near-homeless population, he'd co-written a song for a chart-topping album. Being dumb and naïve, he'd practically given away most of his publishing rights to his co-writer, Jackson Lamont, and settled for a big advance. He never dreamed his song would be nominated for a Grammy. It didn't win, but he received the necessary recognition for his effort. He did have a problem, though. He'd spent that advance money on wine and women and never got around to writing another song. His bedroom had a revolving door, letting women in and out within an hour or two. Sometimes, he hadn't bothered to get their names or ages. What he should've been doing was revolving his butt on that piano bench and cracking out another hit or two.

Despite the dwindling finances, he played one expensive game too many. His life took a downward plunge on the night he decided to play fast and loose with an upcoming successful romance writer named Celeste Francois.

They'd met eleven years ago during a meet and greet for her latest book Mediterranean Rhapsody at the Lavish Publishing Company party in downtown New York City. He was low on money and returned to gigging. That night, he put aside his anger at what Jackson had done, and tucked away the jealousy that that Jackson had succeeded on the strength of Sanjay's creativity. As an olive branch, Jackson reached out to him and extended an offer for Sanjay to play piano, with a five-piece Ska-Rock Funk band that Jackson managed.

Once Sanjay realized that Celeste was a popular and famous author—on a level where he was once as a songwriter—he'd felt a sense of kinship. Sanjay hadn't meant for things to go as far as they did. He felt comfortable in her presence that night and he dismissed his normal preferences. Celeste weighed about ten or fifteen pounds more by his standards. He'd always preferred a female who looked more like a cover girl than one who needed covering up.

After sharing several mixed drinks and nibbling at the food, the conversation turned more personal. She'd loosened up a bit and was more talkative than he since he was keeping his eye on Jackson who had a tendency to skip out with the cash, forcing band members to hunt him down to get their money.

"I've never been married," Celeste had shared. "Barely have opportunities for dating with writing and making deadlines taking up so much time."

"I can certainly appreciate that." He'd told her, half-heartedly.

He remembered the feeling of disappointment after she'd said that and wishing he appreciated that fame could be fleeting. If he'd done like Celeste, he'd gone to possibly playing at Radio City Music Hall with a second shot at a Grammy.

Instead, there he sat at a book release party, having swallowed his pride, and working gigs for his shady writing partner. Jackson, the same backstabbing predator he'd blamed for costing him a Grammy, introducing him to underground parties where so much wickedness went on, Sanjay was repenting simply for the things he'd seen, and not anything he'd done.

"I can't totally blame Jackson," Sanjay whispered, stroking a hand over a Stellar Award that he'd won earlier that year. "I should've fought harder for what I wanted."

Including Celeste Francois.

While his unsuccessful past played in his mind, as it often did these days, Sanjay strolled down the hallway towards his master bedroom. He stopped abruptly and looked into one of the many sculptured mirrors hanging throughout his home. His body stiffened as if it were a statue as he peered deep into the mirror. He had no control and his mind won the battle of remembering that night. He recalled the moment when he'd felt closer to Celeste than any other female company he'd had before. As hard as he tried to forget, Sanjay remembered every word of their conversation.

The loss of her meant he had gained the world, but she still held a small part of his soul.

Cruising' On Desperation

Celeste's run-down slippers clicked on the dirty wooden steps all the way as she maneuvered, holding on to a wobbly bannister. The place was much more ... modest than she'd had at the beginning of her literary career. *No time to write or even feel like writing since I had those twins.*

Nine years later, and the pain from losing her lucrative publishing contract still stung. She wasn't able to provide for her and the girls. Working temp jobs that never led to anything permanent. Celeste took another step and flinched. Her lack of income and the lack of cartilage in her knees were both equally painful. Her kneecaps crunched each time she took a step. "Help me Lord."

Finally, still struggling to catch her breath from the walk down, Celeste bravely held her head high and grabbed at the top of the gate that led out to the sidewalk.

With a shaky hand, she dug into her bra and fetched the last of her money. She blinked back tears as she handed two one-hundred-dollar bills to the foul-smelling man, Devon, who'd she'd once dated because she was cruisin' on desperation. Now, she was disgusted that he'd wanted to go further than she'd wanted. She should've grabbed a knife and did all women a favor.

Her eyes blazed with contempt watching Devon snatch the grocery money and what little would tide her over until something better came along. *I hope you choke on it you monkey.*

He licked his lips, leering as though she'd been some pick-up he paid for with chump change.

Celeste balled her fists trying to rein in her evil thoughts. He wasn't worth it.

Two nights ago, while her twins slept on the floor in a sleeping bag in another room, she'd accepted his offer to stay overnight at his home and then move into the new apartment. She'd felt so abandoned by life, and all that came with it, that she'd gone against her better judgment.

They'd been homeless on and off for the past three years. Her girls had attended too many schools to count. She had to keep one step ahead of Child Protective Services. Now her options were so limited, she'd had to kiss a toad who'd turned into a frog.

So she'd done everything last evening but beg on her knees for a favor. "You know I'm good for it," she'd pled. "I had to hurry and get these girls out of this shelter. I can't keep on living like this and putting these girls in danger. Just let me get them settled in my new place. I'm expecting a check in about a week."

He wasn't satisfied with just being an "old friend" and "helping her out". So retching wasn't all she'd wanted to do when he promised it would be fine while insisting on kissing her deeply for "old times sake." Last night he'd sworn, "Celeste on my Living God above and my dead mama in her cold grave, I'll square everything with my partner." He'd taken it further by adding, "Even if I gotta go into my own pocket or give up my split." Evidently, he had told one Johan's whale of a lie. His mother must've still been breathing instead of six-feet under, and the Living God he had called on didn't resemble the one she knew.

She could've chewed the concrete into dust as she watched those Benjamins meet their fate. Without so much as giving her a sideglance, the foul-smelling turd of a man who resembled a pickled eggplant-shaped brown munchkin, had already began splitting the money between him and the other man with the rabbit ears.

Now she stood on a litter-strewn Brooklyn sidewalk hoping it'd be the last she ever saw him. Celeste felt helpless and discarded by the world and mad enough to wipe every man off the planet.

A pigeon pecked near her run-over house shoes, a reminder that she'd never be a dove.

"Some doggone happy birthday to me," she spat as she turned around. "Lord, if my probation wasn't ending in a few months ..."

QUEEN OF KINGSTON

Don't look at me like that, I told you this would happen.

Samantha stared at Kingston over her parents' dining table, wishing the evening was over. Despite the pleasant surroundings—a dining room filled with expensive furnishings and paintings—the air simmered with nasty undercurrents.

Earlier, she warned him what Mom and Papa's reaction would be to their relationship, but he insisted on coming. "What sense does it make to visit Jamaica and not meet your family?" he'd asked.

She hadn't answered because she understood them, but wasn't ready to deal with their hang-ups and old-fashioned thinking. Kingston's deep-bronze complexion, spiky hair, and almond-shaped eyes would send their stress level into the stratosphere.

Her father, Elias, a stocky, balding man with pale skin, laid his cutlery down and wiped his lips with a napkin. "So, Kingston, do you still have family on the island?"

"My grandmother lives in Clarendon, but my immediate family is in New York." His gaze met hers. "That's where I met Sam."

Sharon DaCosta straightened in her chair and swallowed the Chinese roast chicken as if it had suddenly developed a bitter taste. "*Samantha* insisted on going to university there, against our wishes."

Speaking in a pointed way, Papa glanced around the table. "Aside from getting an education, our daughter came home with radical ideas."

Which includes a relationship with a half-breed Black man.

Nobody said the words, but Sharon DaCosta turned up her nose while pushing aside several blonde strands that escaped from beneath her purple headband decorated with faux pearls. "At least, she kept her gorgeous hair. We were afraid she might've changed it to fit in with her liberal thinking."

She sneered as if Kingston was a bit of refuse one of their spoiled dogs had brought in from the garden.

Michele, her younger sister by two years, rubbed Sam's foot under the table and offered a smile, a gesture of solidarity. She still lived at home, despite being thirty. Their three-story house in Red Hills was the perfect creative environment for her fashion studio, and with her parents' blessing, she commandeered the top floor of the house and came and went as it suited her.

"Sam," Michele said, nodding in their mother's direction, "remember di time when you and Mom wanted to get dem brownish highlights?"

Her sister had never been constrained by societal norms and was classified by the people who knew her as "down to earth," or "roots" in Jamaican terms. Perhaps that was why their father had never pressured her. She was the baby of the family and her colorful personality had revealed itself in her toddler years when she refused to wear disposable diapers and would rip them off as often as their helper caught her and sealed her inside a new one. Now, she had slipped into Patois and added that comment to provoke their father. Sam hoped she didn't have more zingers in her arsenal.

"Enough," Elias' eyes bulged as he seethed. Displeasure turned his complexion corpse-gray. Glancing towards Kingston, he declared. "I said it before and I'll say it again. Your hair is part of your European heritage." Elias took a deep breath as if to allow his meaning to sink in. "Through the centuries, on your mother's side as well as mine, we've kept certain things pure. And pure, they will stay. There will be no brown highlights in your hair or anyplace else."

"So, Papa, does dat still apply to our friends, near and wide?" A smirk appeared on Michele's face and she giggled behind the napkin.

"I believe people should stick to their own kind."

Sam wished Michele wouldn't provoke him. Aside from the subject matter, the use of Patois grated on their father's nerves and the more irritable he became, the more foolishness spewed from his mouth. Not that Michele cared. They had learned Patois at an early age from the household employees and moved fluently between the local language and the Queen's English. When they were children, Papa forbade them to speak broken English, which guaranteed that Michele goaded him by using it when it suited her.

"I'm as Jamaican as anyone else on this island and will not deny that part of my heritage because you're intolerant," she'd told him years ago, to his horror.

Since that time, his attitude and opinion hadn't changed.

Only God knew what Kingston thought of Elias' petulant, shallow declaration. When Sam peeked at Kingston, his bland expression seemed to match Michele's. Perhaps they were kindred spirits. He was certainly taking this display of bad behavior better than Sam, but her perception changed when their eyes met and she felt the heat in his gaze.

Michele's eyes sparkled, and Sam knew she wasn't finished.

With a curious expression in place, she asked, "Do you think Papa meant anything specific? Perhaps, being blonde sets you apart from other affluent people of color in our society." She winked and lowered her head, a habit that surfaced whenever she threw a verbal brick before hiding her hands.

"Doesn't matter to me," Sam replied, despite the rabid way she stabbed the food on her plate. The unpleasant conversation had killed her appetite.

Years ago, Sam grew tired of the weight of her parents' expectations and put as much distance as possible between herself and the family. Even now, her father resented the fact that she got along better with his only brother, Edward, or Ted, as she called him. He had facilitated Sam's flight to freedom and Elias had never forgiven him for it.

"Have you heard from Edward recently?" he asked.

Sam stopped frowning and dropped the fork on her plate with a clang. "As a matter of fact, he spoke with me yesterday."

The mention of his name brought back her anxiety. Sam was working on several stories for the newspaper—one about a brilliant teenager and another about The Castle, a humanitarian organization based in Chicago. Ted was a member of The Castle, but in her research, Sam had stumbled across his name on a list that jarred her. If she could believe it, her uncle had been part of something that might be considered nefarious. But she wouldn't condemn him without speaking to him. He was the first person on her list to contact when she was back in the States.

Rose, their helper, came in to clear the table for dessert. Her cheerful smile and twinkling eyes reminded Sam of the many hours spent with her around the house during her childhood. Whenever she was feeling down, Rose reminded her of the many advantages and blessings she had that other people didn't. She winked at Rose, who stifled a smile.

"Given what you went through in high school, I'm not sure how or why you two connected in this way."

The shock that flickered over Rose's face and dimmed her eyes confirmed that Sharon had abandoned good manners and civility. Not to mention the sudden change in the direction of their conversation, something she reserved for whenever Ted's name was mentioned.

Sam looked directly at her mother. "I'm not one to stay stuck in the past, so ..."

"And I'm not as diplomatic as your mother." Papa pushed his plate aside and leaned back in his oversized chair, one reserved for his girth and status as head of the family.

With an air of authority, he studied each person at the table while his fingers carved a path through a sparse patch of dark hair. He did it when displeased, and now wagged his finger at Samantha.

"The last time you came home, you brought visitors, claiming they were going to be Queens. Delusional. If you don't deal with your past, it will ruin more than your future." With disdain etched on his features, he glanced at Kingston. "I would add that unlearned lessons will taint your present, as well."

The off-hand mention of Cassandra Toussaint, Queen of Curaçao, and Milan Germaine, Queen of Wilmette, roused her annoyance. These were her sister-friends he was disparaging. Members of The Castle with skills and talents her father couldn't even begin to imagine. On top of that, they had a heart for service—unlike her family. Sam's glare found its mark and she didn't hide her anger. Her slender fingers formed a steeple on which she rested her chin.

"Speaking of the past, present, and future," Sam's voice rose with each word. "Have you ever asked Mom if *you* were her *first* choice?"

Elias sprang forward and his weight tilted the chair. "What do you mean?"

His face reddened and a bluish halo appeared around his jowls as though he were about to have a heart attack, or was in the middle of one.

"Has the devil descended in my home?" he snarled as he looked at his wife, then pointed at Samantha. "Sharon, what is she talking about? What does she mean by asking me such a question?"

"The same thing I always mean when posing issues, and you deflect." Sam's voice intensified to match the fervor of her father's. "This time, leave Mom out of this. She may have started it, but this conversation is between me and you, Papa."

"In my home, I decide who a conversation is between. Always has been and always will be." His dictatorial words tore through the air and hung in the bitter silence.

Kingston dropped the linen napkin on the table. "Sir, that is totally uncalled for."

Her father's skin turned a blotchy red. "You, of all people, don't get to tell me what is appropriate in my home."

Pushing back from the table, Kingston rose. "Since it's *me of all people*, and I've figured out this is the way it's going to be, we'll bid you good evening."

Sam and her mother stood at the same time.

"Where are you going?" Sharon asked. Her words said one thing, but a gloss crept across her eyes, turning her question into a plea.

"We're leaving the island tomorrow, anyway. So, it's just as well that I get out of this house tonight."

"I've put up with a lot from you over the years and supported you, even when I didn't believe in what you were doing." Papa tipped his head back to meet Sam's gaze. "But this is different. If you leave here like this, don't come back."

His words had the effect of a throat punch, and tears of frustration seared her eyes. The rash statement that came to her lips couldn't make their way past the tightness in her throat.

Sharon stared at Elias. Her mouth opened and closed several times.

The color drained from Michele's face, leaving her looking like a ghost. The cloud of black hair contrasted with her pasty skin.

Sam turned a desperate gaze on Kingston, whose onyx-colored eyes were closed to slits. She wanted out.

He understood her non-verbal message immediately and buttonholed her father with a searing look that matched Elias' glare—checkmate. Kingston saved her from saying anything she'd regret by gently leading her from the room.

When they stood in the foyer, close to the front door, Kingston cupped her face and whispered, "I'm so sorry. Can you manage?"

Her mother's pair of tan Shih Tzu rushed toward them and swirled around their ankles as if they understood Sam's need for comfort.

She stroked Kingston's cheek and nudged the dogs out of the way. "I'll go upstairs and get my things, then come right down."

His encouraging smile gave Sam the boost she needed to move her heavy feet.

Kingston swiped the tear from the corner of her eye with his thumb and kissed her forehead. "I'll be waiting."

Chapter 2

"The next time my daughter's idiot husband makes you angry, please think before you act."

"Yes, Grandma Esmie." Sam's tone was penitent. Only her grandmother could get that reaction from her.

"That doesn't mean I'm taking their side," she continued. "I'm just upset because you and Kingston didn't come and see me again before flying out."

"I'm sorry. That wasn't intentional." Sam lowered the screen of her laptop and walked around the luxurious suite. "Tell me something though, how come you think so differently from them and you're older."

A few seconds went by before her grandmother said, "I was lucky that when my marriage was arranged, my father understood that I didn't like the man they chose for me. He was a widower and much older than I was. Times were different, but I guess the situation worked out for me because the man I truly loved was also Lebanese and that was acceptable to the family."

"So what happened with Mom?" Sam perched on the sofa and scanned the living room, smiling softly when her gaze landed on the basket of fruits and specialty chocolate Kingston had sent a day after they arrived in Chicago.

They flew from Jamaica to New York's Kennedy International Airport and did something different. Rather than going to their respective homes, they stayed at a hotel in Manhattan. After that chaotic scene at her parents' home, having that intimate time with Kingston in an unfamiliar space was what she wanted. It was also what she needed. The questions she had for Ted could wait until after she repaired the damage her family had done to their relationship. When she had no one else, Kingston stood at her side.

Among their plans was an evening in a Jazz Club on Forty-second Street and visiting some of their old haunts. But once they stepped into the shower together, plans for the Jazz Club faded.

Although Kingston's singing was out of tune and would've caused a cat to scratch out his eyeballs, his love-making with Sam was always in the right key. For the next several hours, he had her singing a different tune in each section of the three room-suite.

Sam crooned "A Whole New World" all the way to "You Make Me Feel Brand New." Just before they'd collapsed from everything they hadn't tried before, Kingston belted, "I Just Can't Wait to Be King."

Two days later, they flew to Chicago based on her need to speak with her uncle. She had continued working on her story and was even more disturbed than she'd been the previous week. Ted had given her permission to occupy one of the bedrooms in his suite at The Castle, and she expected him to return from a business trip this afternoon. Kingston was staying at a friend's apartment nearby.

Sam's mind returned to the conversation when her grandmother said, "Your mother has always been spineless. I only found out after she was engaged to *him* that she had someone else in her life." Her grandmother sighed. "Elias is the strong one in that marriage. Whatever he tells her, Sharon is going to do, no matter how she feels about it. Including trying to run your life and decide who you marry."

Her parents thought it was perfectly all right to make their money off the local population with their movie theater and superstores, but someone of Kingston's color was off-limits.

"It really doesn't matter," she said. "Thank goodness, I don't depend on them for money, so they can take their opinion and stuff it—"

"Careful, Samantha, despite how unenlightened they are, some respect is due."

"Whatever you say, Grandma."

The older woman chuckled, and Samatha pictured the skin around her eyes creasing as she absorbed Sam's snarky response. Grandma Esmie still lived on her own and took care of herself at the ripe old age of eighty-five. The only concession she made to dependency was a housekeeper, who came in twice each week, and the cameras she allowed Sam's father to install inside and outside of her home.

"Give it time, they'll come around," Grandma Esmie said, "Kingston looks like a sensible man. If he's the one, you'll both be all right with each other. I know you have to work, but don't wait too long to call me."

"I won't." Samantha made kissing sounds, then went back to the writing desk to one side of the lounge. She tucked one corner of her lip into her mouth. She had met Kingston at the university, but they remained on the periphery of each other's lives. Four years previously, they crossed paths at the newspaper, where he was a political reporter. At the time, she'd been dabbling in the society pages.

Her qualification in the social sciences made her long for more than tracking social functions and mixing with the glam crowd. When she had the chance to work on human interest stories, she grabbed the opportunity with both hands. One of her articles had a political angle and that's how she re-connected with Kingston, who was also a civil rights lawyer.

He'd filled out and was brawny, with probing, dark eyes that seemed to pierce the depths of her soul. The low stubble on his jaw made her fingers itch to touch his skin.

Was he the one? After these many months she still didn't know, but suspected her reluctance to dive deeper into her emotions came from family expectations. Kingston didn't look like any of her relatives, at least none that were acknowledged. Even as she grew into their relationship, Sam knew her family would be one of their biggest hurdles. The other was Kingston's attitude toward how she did her job. She, also, had the same issue with him.

The door to the suite opened and her uncle walked into the room. Ted was the opposite of his older brother. He was tall and lanky and though his sandy blond hair was thinning, he still turned heads. His olive skin was darker than Elias', but the thin nose with a fleshy tip under thick eyebrows and intense eyes provided a striking family resemblance.

His deep-hazel gaze lit with affection when she met him halfway across the room.

"How's my favorite niece," he asked, as they hugged.

"Fair to fine," she answered. "You know how it is."

"How's the family," he asked, shrugging out of his jacket. He beckoned to the valet, who arrived with his small suitcase.

The uniformed man rolled it into the room and departed when Ted told him it was fine to leave it by the door.

Ted disappeared for a moment, then returned with a bottle of spring water. "So, what brings you here?" he asked, sitting across from her in a Queen Anne wingback chair.

She settled on one of the sofas and curled her legs. "Remember I told you I was doing some research for an article?"

He sipped from the bottle, then nodded. "That sounds like regular stuff."

"Yes, but I came across your name in some documents connected to MiVaxx Incorporated and thought I'd get some clarity from you."

Her imagination might have been working overtime, but Sam thought her uncle stiffened before he grinned and set the bottle on the table next to him. "You're always working on a story. What company did you name just now? I'm on the board of several so forgive me if …" He shrugged and didn't continue.

She enunciated the name slowly, concerned that something was amiss. Why was he acting as if the organization was strange to him, especially since she knew he'd been appointed to the board less than a year ago?

Instead of blurting an accusation, Sam looked away to cover her exasperation. He was lying, and the weight of the unnecessary deceit took her breath away.

"That's fine, *Uncle* Ted, but I know your brain still works." Sam winked. "This is me. Sam. Your *favorite niece*. Spill the tea."

"Spill the tea?" Ted gave a shy grin as he patted the thinning hairs on his head. "Even I, an old man, must give homage to the use of the well-known Internet phrase for telling secrets and revealing the hidden truths."

"Stop dodging. Come on and spill it," Sam wheedled, leaning toward him. "You know that I know that *you* know what I meant the first time."

Sam's usual sing-song way of prodding her uncle to relax and chat failed.

"I promise I will look it up, and if this company ..." Ted rubbed his chin before raising his head. "What was the company name?" He chuckled, and the hand supporting his chin shook slightly. "Your uncle is getting older. My memory is shorter."

Ted was only sixty, so hiding behind age was another clue something was wrong. Despite the impression he gave of being relaxed, Ted couldn't stop fidgeting. He shouldn't be this uncomfortable if he didn't know about the underhanded activity the company was engaged in.

"Remember I won't be here long, so I'd like that information before I leave Chicago."

She studied him closely, waiting for what he'd say next.

OTHER BOOKS BY PAT G'ORGE-WALKER

You might also enjoy other books from my Kensington Publishing catalog:

Don't Blame the Devil
   Sister Betty Says I Do
   Holy Mayhem
   No Ordinary Noel
   Cruisin' on Desperation
   Somebody's Sinning in My Bed
   Somewhat Saved
   Mother Eternal Ann Everlastin's Dead
   Sister Betty! God's Calling You, Again!
   <u>Choices</u>
   Sister Connie Fuse Makes A Grave Mistake

Anthologies

Proverbs for the People
   Spice

OTHER BOOKS BY PAT G'ORGE-WALKER

From Stuck to Limitless
Letter to My Mother

ABOUT PAT G'ORGE-WALKER

Pat G'Orge-Walker is the Essence, and National bestselling and award-winning author of the Christian fiction Sister Betty comedy series, as well as contemporary fiction, Women's issues, Romance novels. The novels published by Kensington/Dafina that fearlessly burrow into issues sometimes labeled taboo or left unsaid by Christian and secular community without subverting the Good News or watering down the potency of its message. She is also a contributor to New York Times anthologies and a three-time AALAS winner for Comedy as well as several other prestigious awards. Pat, a PK, has quietly soaked up material from her father's Baptist congregation and her mother's Pentecostal assembly to create and keep her audiences howling with laughter, performing nationwide and on the high seas with her One-Woman comedy show, "Sister Betty! God's Calling You!"

Before entering the Publishing arena, she was a recording industry veteran working promotion/marketing with Epic, Columbia and Def Jam records. And, before that, she sang with Arlene Smith and the Chantels (Maybe, He's Gone, Look in My Eyes.)

Today, she is constantly looking to connect further with her reader and fan base. www.pgorgewalker.com as The First Lady of Gospel Comedy forges a successful career as author and comedian. She currently resides in NC.

Find her on the web and social media:
    https://sociatap.com/sisterbetty/
    Pat G'Orge-Walker – www.pgorgewalker.com

www.ingramcontent.com/pod-product-compliance
Lightning Source LLC
Chambersburg PA
CBHW011614290426
44110CB00020BA/2586